THE
CHOW CHOW

by Charlotte Wilcox

Consultant:
Mary L. Wuest
Licensed AKC Breeder/Judge

CAPSTONE
HIGH-INTEREST
BOOKS

an imprint of Capstone Press
Mankato, Minnesota

Capstone High-Interest Books are published by Capstone Press
151 Good Counsel Drive, P.O. Box 669, Mankato, Minnesota 56002
http://www.capstone-press.com

Library of Congress Cataloging-in-Publication Data
Wilcox, Charlotte.
    The chow chow/by Charlotte Wilcox.
    p. cm.—(Learning about dogs)
    Includes bibliographical references (p. 45) and index.
    Summary: Introduces the history, development, uses, and care of this
fluffy dog breed, credited with inspiring the creation of the teddy bear.
    ISBN 0-7368-0159-6
    1. Chow chow (Dog breed)—Juvenile literature. [1. Chow chow
(Dog breed). 2. Dogs.] I. Title II. Series: Wilcox, Charlotte. Learning
about dogs.
SF429.C5W55   1999
636.72—dc21   98-37630
                                                                    CIP
                                                                    AC

Editorial Credits

Timothy Halldin, cover designer; Sheri Gosewisch and Kimberly Danger,
    photo researchers

Photo Credits

Betty Crowell, 26
Cheryl A. Ertelt, 9, 14, 25, 38
Ingrid Mårn Wood, 10, 33
Kent and Donna Dannen, 16, 20, 23, 37
Mark Raycroft, 4, 6, 13, 19, 31, 40-41
Photobank, Inc./Lacz Lemoine, cover
Photo Network/Gay Bumgarner, 28; Henry Kaiser, 34

2 3 4 5 6 05 04 03 02

Table of Contents

Quick Facts about the Chow Chow

Description

Height: Chow Chows stand 17 to 20 inches (43 to
                 51 centimeters) tall. Height is measured
                 from the ground to the withers. The
                 withers are the tops of the shoulders.

Weight: Male Chow Chows weigh 55 to 70 pounds
                 (25 to 32 kilograms). Females weigh 45 to
                 60 pounds (20 to 27 kilograms).

Physical features:	Most Chow Chows have thick, fluffy hair. A dog's hair is called its coat. Some Chows have smooth coats. Chow Chows' tongues and mouths are black. Chow Chows' tails curve over their backs. Their back legs do not bend like the back legs of other dogs. This makes them run stiffly.
Color:	Chows Chows' coats can be one of five main colors. Red coats can be from light gold to deep red-brown. Cinnamon coats can be from light tan to brown. Blue coats are dark blue-gray. Chow Chows' coats also can be black or cream.

Development

Place of origin:	Chow Chows came from China.
History of breed:	Chow Chows descended from ancient war dogs of Asia.
Numbers:	The American Kennel Club registers about 10,000 Chow Chows each year. Register means to record a dog's breeding record with an official club. The Canadian Kennel Club registers about 350 Chow Chows each year.

Uses

Most Chow Chows in North America are pets. A few people use them as hunting or guard dogs.

Chapter 1
The Teddy Bear Dog

It is easy to spot Chow Chows. People recognize these dogs by their unusual faces. Most Chow Chows have a large amount of fluffy hair around their necks. This hair is called a ruff. Chow Chows are often called Chows for short.

Chow Chows remind many people of lions or bears. Some people think that Chow Chows' ruffs make them look like small lions. Other people think they look like little bears. Chows have black tongues and mouths. Some polar and Asian bears have black tongues like Chows. Only one other dog breed has a black

Some people compare Chow Chows to lions or bears.

tongue. This is the shar-pei. It is similar to the Chow Chow.

The Teddy Bear Legend

Some people say the Chow Chow has a face like a teddy bear. A legend says the first teddy bear was made to look like a Chow Chow. No one knows if this story from the past is true.

In the 1800s, Queen Victoria of England had a Chow Chow puppy. She took it everywhere she went. Some of the queen's friends did not like the dog. They thought a queen should not carry around a dog.

The queen's friends paid a dressmaker to make a stuffed Chow Chow. This toy looked just like the queen's puppy. People thought the toy Chow Chow looked like a bear. Other dressmakers began making them. They called them teddy bears.

Most people believe a different teddy bear story. They think that teddy bears were named after Theodore Roosevelt. Roosevelt's nickname was Teddy. He was president of the United States from 1901 to 1909.

Chow Chows have a black tongue.

Chapter 2

The Beginnings of the Breed

The Chow Chow is one of the world's oldest dog breeds. Some scientists believe Chows first came from China more than 2,000 years ago. Others believe the Chow originated in the Arctic area of Asia as long as 3,000 years ago. They think the Chow next came to Mongolia, Siberia, and China.

One Chinese legend tells of large war dogs from central Asia. People said the dogs looked like lions and had black tongues. The Chinese people called these dogs "bear dogs."

Many people believe Chow Chows first came from Asia.

Chow Chow pictures appear on pottery and sculpture found in China. These pieces of art are about 2,000 years old. The pictures show people using Chow Chows to hunt birds, tigers, and bears. One Chinese ruler owned 5,000 Chow Chows about 1,300 years ago. He trained 10,000 men to hunt with them.

Chows once did many kinds of work for people. The explorer Marco Polo was the first European to report about Chows. Polo went to China in the 1200s. He saw Chinese people using Chows to pull sleds. The dogs also pulled carts and carried packs.

The Chow Chow also had other uses in China. Chow Chows herded animals and guarded property. Some Chinese people raised Chow Chows for food and clothing. The meat was considered a special treat. Some people used Chows' thick fur to make clothing.

The Chow Chow's Name

Chow means "food" in the Cantonese language. This language is spoken in China.

In China, some people used Chow Chows as guard dogs.

Chinese people did not call their dogs Chows. They called them bear dogs, black-tongued dogs, or wolf dogs.

English sailors probably named the dogs Chow Chows. Many English ships sailed to China in the 1700s. The sailors bought jewelry, household goods, and food from the Chinese. They brought these goods back to England to sell. The sailors learned a few Chinese words. They began to call all Chinese goods chow chow.

In the late 1700s, English sailors began to buy the bear dogs. They called the dogs chow chow like other Chinese goods. Sailors first brought Chow Chows to England in 1781. English people liked the dogs. The English also called the dogs Chow Chows.

English sailors began to buy Chow Chows in the late 1700s.

Chapter 3

The Development of the Breed

The first Chow Chows brought to England were not pets. They lived in a zoo in London. But English people were very interested in the unusual dogs. Chow Chows soon became pets in English homes.

During the 1800s, Chow Chows became more and more popular in England. In 1865, Queen Victoria was given a Chow brought to England from China. Soon many people wanted to have a dog like the queen's. In 1895, a group of English people started the first Chow Chow club.

Chow Chows became popular in England during the 1800s.

Chow Popularity Grows

Interest in Chow Chows began to grow. People in other European countries and in North America bought Chows in England. The Chow Chow Club of America began in 1906. But Chows still were not common in North America. They also were expensive. One prize Chow from England cost its American owner almost $10,000.

During the 1900s, the Chow became more popular in the United States and Canada. U.S. president Calvin Coolidge had two Chows. Coolidge was president of the United States from 1923 to 1929. Coolidge's Chows were named Tiny Tim and Blackberry. They lived in the White House while Coolidge was president.

During the 1900s, Chow Chows became more popular in the United States and Canada.

Chapter 4
The Chow Chow Today

Today, there are few Chow Chows left in China. Most live in Europe, North America, and Australia. Chows are no longer used for food or clothing. Most Chows live with families as pets.

In the 1980s, Chow Chows were one of North America's most popular dogs. People registered nearly 50,000 Chow Chows in 1986. Register means to record a dog's breeding record with an official dog club. Today, the American Kennel Club registers about 10,000

Most Chow Chows today live with families as pets.

Chows each year. The Canadian Kennel Club registers about 350 Chows each year.

Features of a Chow Chow

Chow Chows have unusual faces. Their faces are similar to bears' faces. Some people think Chows appear to be frowning. This does not mean they are angry or unhappy. Their faces naturally look this way.

Chow Chow puppies are born with pink tongues. Their tongues and mouths turn black after about eight weeks. Their noses also are black.

Chows' back legs do not bend like the back legs of other dogs. This makes them run in a stiff way. Chows' tails are curved over their backs.

Chow Chows are medium-sized dogs. They stand 17 to 20 inches (43 to 51 centimeters) tall. Height is measured from the ground to the withers. The withers are the tops of the shoulders. Male Chows weigh 55 to 70 pounds (25 to 32 kilograms). Females weigh 45 to 60 pounds (20 to 27 kilograms).

Smooth-coated Chow Chows have shorter hair than rough-coated Chow Chows.

The Chow Chow has a square-shaped body. This means its length is the same as its height. A Chow that is 18 inches (46 centimeters) tall has a body about 18 inches (46 centimeters) long.

Two Coat Types
Chow Chows can have two different types of coats. Their coats can be rough or smooth.

Rough-coated Chows have thick, fluffy hair. They have a longer ruff around their necks. This makes them look like small lions. Most Chow Chows have rough coats.

Smooth-coated Chows look similar to rough-coated Chows. But they have shorter hair and they do not have ruffs.

Chow Chows can be one of five main colors. They can be red, black, blue, cinnamon, or cream. Red and black are the most common Chow colors. Red coats range from light gold to deep red-brown. Cinnamon ranges from light tan to brown. Blue is dark blue-gray. Both rough-coated and smooth-coated Chows come in these same five colors.

Some Chow Chows have cream-colored coats. Cream Chows often have brown noses as adults. Dog clubs do not allow these dogs in shows. Chows must have black noses, tongues, and mouths to enter shows. But cream Chows still make good pets.

Red and black are the most common Chow Chow colors.

Chapter 5
Owning a Chow

People once used Chow Chows for hunting, herding animals, and guarding property. Today, most Chows are household pets. But they have kept some of their original character. They can be pushy or rough with strangers. They need good training to keep them under control.

Usually it is easy to train Chows. Most Chows are smart. People can housebreak Chow puppies by the time the puppies are 8 weeks old. Chows also quickly learn how to walk on a leash.

Chow Chows sometimes act more like cats than dogs. They like to have people around.

Chow Chows need good training to keep them under control.

But they do not always like people to get close to them. Chows do not always like to be hugged. They tend to be quiet and keep to themselves. They also do not like to get wet.

Chow Chows must be socialized to make good pets. Chows must be socialized when they are puppies. Owners socialize Chow puppies by getting them used to people and other pets.

Keeping a Chow Chow

Chow Chows are good house dogs. They do not need a great deal of exercise. They can be content and healthy in a city apartment. They enjoy walks outside. But they do not like to sleep outside. Chows need shelter from sun, wind, rain, and snow.

Chows' coats keep them warm in cold weather. But they must never get too hot. Too much heat can make them sick.

A Chow Chow needs its own place inside a house. A basket, dog bed, or dog crate works well. A dog crate is similar to a cage.

Chow Chows must be socialized when they are puppies.

The bottom of the crate should be covered with a blanket or pillow. The crate should be placed in a quiet corner. It should be away from drafts or direct heat.

If a Dog Gets Lost

Dogs must always have identification. This helps owners find their dogs if the dogs get lost. Some owners have their names and telephone numbers stamped on their dogs' collars. Others have their dogs tattooed. These marks on the dogs' skin contain information about how to contact the dogs' owners.

Today, some owners have microchips put under their dogs' skin. This computer chip is the size of a grain of rice. A veterinarian must put in the microchip. Veterinarians are trained to treat sick or injured animals. The microchip can be read by a computer. It tells the owner's name, address, and telephone number. It also can give other information about the dog.

Chow Chows do not need a great deal of exercise.

Feeding a Chow Chow

The Chinese people did not feed their dogs meat. They fed them rice. Today, Chow Chows cannot eat much meat. Too much meat can give them skin problems. Rice, eggs, and cottage cheese are good foods for Chows.

Kibble makes a good diet for Chow Chows. This dry dog food is inexpensive and easy to keep. But some Chows cannot eat kibble dry. Dry kibble can cause too much gas to form in these dogs' stomachs. Chows can die from this condition. Kibble must be mixed with warm water for these dogs.

Chows eat various amounts of food. An adult Chow may eat 1 pound (.5 kilograms) of kibble a day. People can divide this food into morning and evening meals. People also may feed Chows just once a day in the evening. It is important not to feed dogs too much.

Some foods are dangerous for dogs. Chocolate can be poisonous to some dogs. Dogs also can get sick from spicy or fatty foods. Small or sharp bones are not good

Chow Chows cannot eat much meat. Rice, eggs, and cottage cheese are good foods for Chows.

Chow Chows' coats keep them cool in summer and warm in winter.

for dogs. They can injure dogs' stomachs. Fish and chicken bones especially are unsafe for dogs.

Dogs need plenty of fresh water. Water should be available to them at all times. They should drink at least three times a day.

Grooming

All Chow Chows need to be groomed. Owners need to keep their Chows neat and clean.

Chows also like to clean themselves. Many Chows lick their faces after eating. Chows do not have body odor like many other dogs.

Chows' thick coats should be combed or brushed regularly. Chows shed much of their hair in the spring. They also lose some hair during the rest of the year. Their coats must be brushed at least twice a week. Their ruffs must be carefully combed. Chow Chows' coats should never be clipped. Their coats keep the dogs cool in summer and warm in winter.

Chow Chows cannot stay clean if their surroundings are dirty. Their beds and blankets should be washed often. Owners should give their Chows baths when they get dirty. This can be difficult because Chows do not like to get wet.

Dog owners need to care for their dogs in other ways. Some dogs' toenails can get too long. Owners then must trim them. Chow Chows also need to have their teeth cleaned. Owners can buy special toothpastes and toothbrushes for dogs. Dogs' ears should be cleaned once a month. Veterinarians can show owners how to do these grooming tasks.

Health Care

Chow Chows have few health problems. Some Chows have problems with their eyes. Their eyelids can turn in toward the eyeball. Dogs with this problem get more tears than are normal in their eyes. Veterinarians can treat this problem.

Dogs need shots every year to prevent illnesses such as rabies and distemper. They need pills to guard against heartworms. These tiny worms are spread by mosquitoes. They enter a dog's heart and slowly destroy it. Dogs also need a yearly checkup for other types of worms.

Owners must check their dogs for ticks every day during warm weather. Some of these small insects carry Lyme disease. This serious illness affects both animals and humans. Owners also must check their dogs for fleas,

Chow Chows have few health problems.

lice, and mites. These tiny insects live in dogs' fur.

Chow Chows need special treatment during operations. Chows sometimes stop breathing when given anesthetics. These drugs block pain. Veterinarians give anesthetics to animals before operations.

Finding a Chow Chow

Chow Chows can be difficult to buy. Healthy Chows often are expensive. Pet stores often sell Chows that are not healthy or socialized.

The best Chows usually are sold through responsible breeders. Breeders raise dogs to sell directly to people looking for pets. Show breeders are dependable sources for healthy dogs.

People who want Chow Chows should contact the nearest Chow Chow club. These clubs help people find good breeders.

Some people can find Chows through rescue shelters. Rescue shelters find homes for homeless dogs. They sometimes offer older dogs for adoption. Shelters usually charge lower prices than breeders charge. Some shelter dogs are free. Many rescued dogs already are trained. A well-trained Chow can make a fine pet.

Chow Chow clubs can help people find good breeders.

Ears

Muzzle

Chest

Ruff

Forequarters

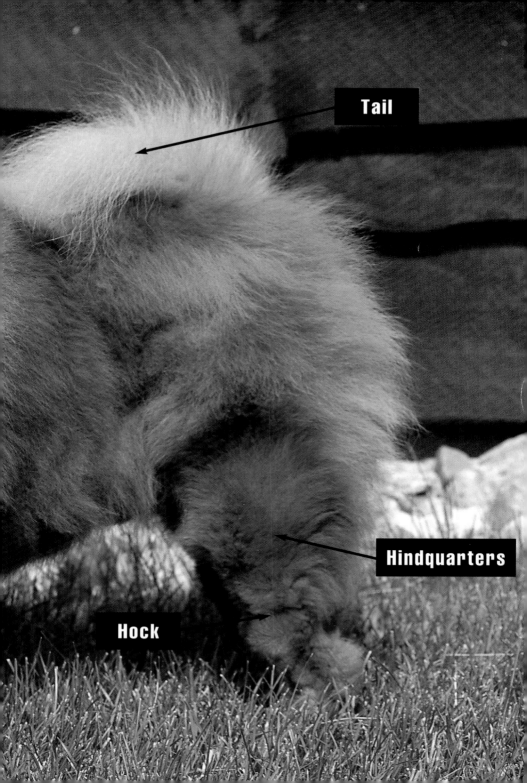

Tail

Hindquarters

Hock

Quick Facts about Dogs

Dog Terms

A male dog is called a dog. A female dog is called a bitch. A young dog is called a puppy until it is 1 year old. A newborn puppy is called a whelp until it no longer needs its mother's milk. A family of puppies born at one time is called a litter.

Life History

Origin:	All dogs, wolves, coyotes, and dingoes descended from a single, wolf-like species. Humans trained dogs throughout history.
Types:	There are about 350 official dog breeds in the world. Dogs come in different sizes and colors. Adult dogs weigh from 2 pounds (1 kilogram) to more than 200 pounds (91 kilograms). They range from 6 inches (15 centimeters) to 36 inches (91 centimeters) tall.
Reproductive life:	Dogs mature at 6 to 18 months. Puppies are born two months after breeding. A female can have two litters per year. An average litter has three to six puppies. Litters of 15 or more puppies are possible.
Development:	Newborn puppies cannot see or hear. Their ears and eyes open one to two weeks after birth. Puppies try to walk when they are 2 weeks old. Their teeth begin to come in when they are about 3 weeks old.
Life span:	Dogs are fully grown at 2 years. They can live 15 years or longer with good care.

The Dog's Super Senses

Smell:

Dogs have a strong sense of smell. It is many times stronger than a human's. Dogs use their noses more than their eyes and ears. They recognize people, animals, and objects just by smelling them. They may recognize smells from long distances. They also may remember smells for long periods of time.

Hearing:

Dogs hear better than people do. Dogs can hear noises from long distances. They can also hear high-pitched sounds that people cannot hear.

Sight:

Dogs' eyes are farther to the sides of their heads than people's are. They can see twice as wide around their heads as people can.

Touch:

Dogs enjoy being petted more than almost any other animal. They also can feel vibrations from approaching trains or the beginning of earthquakes or storms.

Taste:

Dogs do not have a strong sense of taste. This is partly because their sense of smell overpowers their sense of taste. It also is partly because they swallow food too quickly to taste it well.

Navigation:

Dogs often can find their way home through crowded streets or across miles of wilderness without guidance. This is a special ability that scientists do not fully understand.

Words to Know

anesthetic (an-iss-THET-ik)—a drug that blocks pain; anesthetics can make Chows sick.

groom (GROOM)—to brush, clean, and take care of an animal

kibble (KIB-uhl)—dry dog food

Lyme disease (LIME duh-ZEEZ)—an illness carried by ticks that causes weakness, pain, and sometimes heart and nerve problems in animals and humans

microchip (MYE-kroh-chip)—a computer chip about the size of a grain of rice; a computer chip can be put under a dog's skin to help identify it.

register (REJ-uh-stur)—to record a dog's breeding record with an official kennel club

ruff (RUHF)—a ring of long hair around a dog's neck

veterinarian (vet-ur-uh-NER-ee-uhn)—a person trained to treat sick or injured animals

To Learn More

American Kennel Club. *The Complete Dog Book for Kids*. New York: Howell Book House, 1996.

Driscoll, Laura. *All About Dogs and Puppies*. All Aboard Books. New York: Grosset & Dunlap, 1998.

Hansen, Ann Larkin. *Dogs*. Popular Pet Care. Minneapolis: Abdo & Daughters, 1997.

Rosen, Michael J. *Kids' Best Dog Book*. New York: Workman, 1993.

You can read articles about Chow Chows in *AKC Gazette*, *Chow Life*, *Dog Fancy*, and *Dog World* magazines.

Useful Addresses

American Kennel Club
5580 Centerview Drive, Suite 200
Raleigh, NC 27606

Canadian Kennel Club
89 Skyway Avenue, Suite 100
Etobicoke, ON M9W 6R4
Canada

Chow Chow Adoption Center
9828 East County A
Janesville, WI 53546

The Chow Chow Club, Inc.
P.O. Box 540
Seaford, NY 11783

Chow Chow Fanciers of Canada
32829 Bakerview Avenue
Mission, BC V2V 2P8
Canada

Internet Sites

American Kennel Club
http://www.akc.org

Canadian Kennel Club
http://www.ckc.ca

The Chow Chow Club, Inc.
http://www.chowclub.org

Digital Dog
http://www.digitaldog.com

Dog Fancy On-Line
http://www.dogfancy.com/default.asp

Dog World Online
http://www.dogworldmag.com

Index